Confessions

Paradox

BookLeaf
Publishing

India | USA | UK

For Xiao Zhan who knows not of my existence
but still managed to fill my world with stardust
and euphoria.

For you, whose soul might be in need of
healing, to find solace in a beautiful journey of
waiting and unrequited love.

Encounter

You donned red and black when I first met you.
You looked defeated.
Your heart was severely broken,
    and mine broke into million pieces
        because I cannot mend yours.

Your soul was mirrored in your eyes
        – out in the open for the world to see.
You were beautiful
    even when enveloped in despair.
It was then that I knew,
        I will walk worlds and universes,
            swim depths and darkness for you.
Your smile back then,
        painful and broken as it was,
            cannot be erased from my memories.

Oath

The love songs on the radio remind me of you.
Nostalgia and disappointment
       plagued my senses with your memory.
In your presence I am embraced with wonder,
       you aroused my long-standing inertia.

Tormented by my anonymity,
       I gathered fortitude from your laughter
              – soft rain and gentle wind
                     amidst the chaos of a thunderstorm.
Despite my absence in your reality,
       I shall stand by you.
Through every catastrophe, I shall be here.

Unseen

The world outside is dark and gloomy.
Stuck in bed – unwell and melancholic,
    I found myself thinking of you.
You breached my thoughts
    and stubbornly plagued my imaginations.
In daydream, I caught myself wondering,
    Is your heart safe and unbroken?
The world has potential for cruelty.
Humanity is double sided,
    readily blinded by temperament.
Misdirected, society has capacity to viciousness.
If I can protect your gentleness from resentment,
    I would do so without hesitation

If only I could. But, I can't.

All I can do is write to you,
    frivolous letters you will never read.
Orchestrate declaration of affections,
    prepare mediums you will never see.
Serenade your soul with melodies of comfort,
    music and lyrics you will never hear.
Nameless behind make-believe,
    I stand my ground and stand by you.

Remedy

Life fractured my soul today.
My heart is crippled, weakened in anguish.
Breathing is an endeavor,
        a struggle against the tightness in my chest.
My heart is broken,
        I don't know where to start fixing it.

So, I put my playlist on shuffle.
I listened to your voice filter through.
Your calming voice is as beautiful
        as it was in my memories.
 Your heart-warming melodies
        soothed the pandemonium within.

You really are my remedy.
You inspire me endlessly.

As I sit here listening, I thought of you.
Maybe tomorrow, my sun will rise once again.
Your eloquence has been my saving grace.
You are too good to be true, I am awed by you.

Greed

On a day such as this,
    I want to be by your side.
I want to look into your eyes
    and take your hand in mine.
Assure you that there is light
    at the end of this long, dark tunnel.
I wanted to take you away from reality,
    surround you with beauty and laughter.

Your absence left me pondering.
I wonder if believing in you is adequate.
I wish there is something more that I can do.
There isn't and it's agonizing.

I am waiting for you
    – for your sunny smile to fill up my world
      with everything warm and breathtaking.
I am here waiting for you to come back to me.

You are not alone.
All you must do is look up – I am here.

Longing

I want to know everything about you.
Things that make you happy,
    those that break your heart.
Flavors that you enjoy,
    melodies that calm your soul.
I want to be the person who knows you best,
    I know that I'll never be.

I saw snippets of some of your old memories.
Your smile is a firefly show on a summer night,
    – alluring, soft and enlightening.
Hundreds of tiny starlights in the darkness.
Your honey toned skin is heart-warming.
Even back then, you lit up the gloom.

It saddens me to remember.
I'll never be able to wax poetic of your soul,
    nor can I hold your hand to uplift your spirit.
Our realities are not meant to mingle.

April Fool's

A soft, sweet refrain is serenading me.
Words of longing and waiting
 are stirring something within my soul.
There's a peculiar feeling in my chest
 – a sense of melancholy creeping in.

Ah, I am missing you!

Waiting for you is saccharine.
A blissful torment, somewhat bittersweet.
But, if on your return,
 that smile of yours shall be as incandescent
 as Pleiades in the Taurus constellation
 – then, my dear,
 the wait will be worth it.

Assertion

The world underestimates
     the feelings I nourish for you.
Chemical reactions faded, yet here I am.
Sometimes, I contemplate
     on snippets of your frozen memories.
As moonlight shines through my window
     and shadows invade corners of my life,
        I think of my past and my future.

You are instilled in every part of it – always.
Every frame of memories.
Every wishful thinking.
Replays of past turning points.
Futures yet to come.

They assume my affections are trifling.
Melancholy fills my soul.
How lamentable!
But I have a lifetime,
     a lifetime should be long enough.

Magpie

A bird of black and white dwells on the balcony,
      staring out towards the hinterland.
Singing arias of varied pitches,
      somewhat desperate assonance.
The melodies sound woeful
      – filled with longing and despair.
Hearts stirring, thoughts wandering.
My entirety suffused with thoughts of you.
I find solace in my anticipation of your return.
When you are ready, reach out.
I am here.

Sandman

Slumber evaded me.
The sandman skipped the route
in which I was waiting.
I laid in bed – awake, uncertain.

Eyes wandered around the pitch blackness.
Darkness reigned,
the moon cloaked within the shadows.
Between the gaps in the curtains,
I scrutinize shimmering constellations
– ablaze, proud, and unwavering.

Sentiments roared so vehemently.
Overwhelming. Heart rending.
Mayhem deep within my soul.
Amidst the chaos, you came to me.
The memory of your smile
vanquished my innermost turmoil.
Undisclosed war urged to an impasse.

My soul stilled. My heart softened.
You filled my senses, my every breath.
As dawn chased away the darkness,
your voice lulled me to rest.

You are a specter

– a reality that cannot exist next to mine.
Your dominion over my existence is unnerving
The feelings I hold for you are frightening.

Unrestrained

The delicate melody of the *guqin* and *dizi*
    played softly in the background.
Libretto of a life permeated with paradoxes.
Fragments of dazzling moments and tragedies.
Resignations and yearnings.
Death and second chances.

Love lost and found.

While the melodies waltzed with the verses,
    I felt my heart falter.
Mellow voice stirred complex emotions
    from the deepest recesses of my soul
        – empathy, desire, love, melancholy.

Your silence is deafening,
    thunderous in the wake of your laugh.
Nevertheless, I am listening.
Quietly anticipating your return,
    finding solace in your blinding smile.

My existence burns with the eloquence of yours.
Waiting for you is as easy as breathing,
    You will always be worth waiting for.

Manifesto

Letters dedicated to you saturate the crevices
     of my mundane existence.
Journal of sentiments forever out of your grasp.
Drabbles of affections unknown to you
       – encouragements, unfulfilled promises,
         one-sided conversations.

A stash of secret literature.
Musings of someone who exists parallel to you
     – never meeting, equidistant.
A manifesto you will never discover.

My soul is overflowing with affection.
You challenge my deepest resolve,
    confront my truths with conviction.
Overpowered and bursting in the seams,
    I had no choice but to write.

So I did.

Winter Lemons

Winter has arrived.
Icy draft seeping through my bones
      – welcoming, refreshing, friendly.
The coldness from within is unwelcome
      – desolating, numbing, imposing.
Life showered me lemons in abundance
Pitchers of lemonades fill my fridge.
Lemon tarts are baking in the oven.
I am spent, utterly exhausted.
Fighting is wearying and my soul is breaking.

Then I look up, and there you are.

You and your smile
      that rivals the warmth of a thousand suns.
You and your beautiful clear eyes
      transfixed to an inconspicuous future
        and imagined intention.
You and your unyielding tenacity
      to contest an impregnable adversary
        – indifference and antagonism.
Standing behind you,
      whose shoulders are set straight and proud,
        How can I let myself surrender?

Broken Silence

You broke your silence
       – blue skies and swimming whales.
My heart is fragmented
       – soul ailing and vision obscured.
In your presence, the clouds have lifted.
Your scenery unshackled me from melancholy.
You inspire me, motivate me, encourage me.
The way you touch my soul cannot be explained
       – something akin to magic and unicorn.
You unraveled my perspective
       and revealed a different landscape.

Selene

The full moon dominates the night sky
        – bright, beautiful, bewitching.
Clouds attempt to cover its brilliance.
It remained undaunted.
Humanity romanticizes Earth's Selene.
It emanates elegance and grandeur.
The darkness lightened by its mere existence.

You are the full moon in my midnight sky.
Even in crepuscule, you luminesce.
You are blinding,uplifting, heartening.
You radiate in the gloom of blackness,
Remaining incandescent in the arrival of Aurora.

I am spellbound by your heart.
Your mind takes my breath away.
You are a breathing testament
        that even darkness is ephemeral,
            that there is beauty in darkness.

Old Friend

Solitude embraced me like an old friend
        – familiar, estranged.
Tonight, it sneaked in and grasped my core.
The corners of my mind quivered,
        the alcove of my consciousness shuddered.
Solitude called the Winter Queen
        and invited her to my temple.
Once again, I am unmoored
        – adrift in an expanse of my own creation.

Then you came crashing through the tempest,
        lit up my darkened sky with your smile.
Your whisper echoed unhindered,
        aroused from the deepest alcove
                of my awareness.
Visions of your laugh fractured my phantasies.
I sought after you in pages of stilled memories,
        snapshots affirming your actuality.
Grasped on any testament of your existence.

The cobwebs of my lonesomeness
        expelled from the ridges of my mind.
The hail settled, the cold warmed.
Your presence chased my old friend away.

Once again, I am centered

– tethered, conquered, moored.

Twilight

Half of the world is asleep.
The other half is waking up.
Mine is kept illuminated
          by glaring fluorescent lights.
My hands dabbled with blood.
Some splattered on my pale, blue scrubs.
The heart monitor is beeping loudly
          – strong, steady and grounding.
Stable numbers on the screen.
As I washed the red stain off,
          I thought of life – short and sweet.
There is beauty in its impermanence.

I thought of love – exquisite, piercing, enduring.
I thought of you.

Your absence is heart rending,
          a lucid voice in the gaps of existence.
You are imperative to my being.
It was inevitable in the dawn of your smile
          – warm and blinding.

If you are anchored and safeguarded
          through this never-ending albatross,
                    there is nothing else that I desire.
Whatever keeps you moored is irrelevant.

Your well being is all that matters.
And when you are ready,
            turn around, I'll be waiting.

Deities

Despite the shadow of a realist in my soul,
      I am a romantic.
I mushroom under the ephemeral,
        chase transient beautiful cherry blossoms
           and devour the notions of thaumaturgy.
I stand in defiance of mediocrity,
        the truth I speak is unrelenting.
If I so desire, I am unyielding and immovable.

Ever since I saw you in hues of black and red,
        weeping for all that has been lost,
           I decided to believe in you.
My faith in you will never waver,
        unbothered by uncertainties of realities.

I will stand my ground and dig my heels.
I will bite my tongue when needed
        and contend when necessary.
But I will never leave your side.
You will never be abandoned.
You will never be alone
Seven thousand four hundred kilometers,
        the distance between me and you,
          is miniscule and irrelevant.

I will hold your hand securely if you ask,

safeguard your heart from rancor.
Your enemies shall be mine
        and I will face battlefields by your side.
If you need strength, I will be strong for you.
If love is what you desire,
        I have more than ten lifetimes worth.

If time is what you require,
        I'll befriend Tai Sui, Li Su, and Yang Xin.
You can have all the time you need.
Fate will be your valuable companion.
Even Kan-Laon will be by your side.
When your seclusion comes to an end,
        ready to face the spotlight again,
                I will be where I was when you left.

Seventh Eve

The magpies of mythology gathered,
    star-crossed lovers began their voyage,
      Heavenly River traversed.
The brightest star in the constellation of Lyra
    embraced the luminous point of Aquila.
A year of separation passed,
    Vega and Altair entwined at last.
The cowherd and weaver girl side by side,
    the Milky Way glowed all around.
The magpies brought the ill-fated together,
    their feathered wings escorted you to me.
My composure faltered in your presence.
The entirety of my being expanded with warmth,
    my soul exploded into starlight.
Each piece alight with exhilaration,
    glowing with sentiments unlocked
      by the ghost of your smile.
Like a *fortissimo* out of composition,
    ravaging the ensemble of my existence
      – a crescendo, andante, diminuendo.
Harmonizing to uplift me to a state of Euphoria.
You are the orchestra,
    the symphony I want to listen to
      until the end of time.

Homeless

My heart is in pieces
        – fragmented beyond repair.
I can feel it subtly beating,
        the gnawing pain makes me breathless.

My soul is shattered,
        scattered on the bedroom floor.
How do I glue myself together?
Where do I start gathering the pieces?
What can I do through the blur
        and the mist shrouding my senses?

He was my 'home',
        one that I was fighting to keep.
But he gave up the fight
        and suddenly I was left homeless.

Then you tumbled
        into the frame of my existence,
Red scarf and obsidian hair
        sprinkled with flakes of alabaster snow.
Your crimson smile
        besieged my deepest fantasies.
The fervor of your passion
        challenged my insecurities.
Your compassion thawed

the shackles of grief
        tormenting my being.

Once again, here I am
        – stronger, loved, and 'home'.